AWESOME ARMORED ANIMALS

CAIMANS, GHARIALS, ALLIGATORS, AND CROCODILES

Bethany Baxter

PowerKiDS press.

New York

Published in 2014 by The Rosen Publishing Group, Inc.
29 East 21st Street, New York, NY 10010

First Edition

Editor: Julia Quinlan
Book Design: Greg Tucker
Layout Design: Colleen Bialecki

Photo Credits: Cover Juan Garcia/Shutterstock.com; p. 4 neelsky/Shutterstock.com; p. 5 Eric Gevaert/Shutterstock.com; p. 6 Delmas Lehman/Shutterstock.com; p. 7 Mogens Trolle/Shutterstock.com; p. 8 oattume/Shutterstock.com; p. 9 (top) Merial Land/Oxford Scientific/Getty Images; p. 9 (bottom) Roel Meijer/Photographers Choice RF/Getty Images; p. 10 Robert Llewellyn/Workbook Stock/Getty Images; p. 11 e2dan/Shutterstock.com; p. 12–13 Matt Hansen Photography. Dynamic Wildlife Photography/Flickr/Getty Images; p. 14 hxdbzxy/Shutterstock.com; p. 15 Bob Elsdale/The Image Bank/Getty Images; p. 16 Andy Rouse/The Image Bank/Getty Images; p. 17 (top) Jupiterimages/Photos.com/Thinkstock; p. 17 (bottom) Paul Soulders/The Image Bank/Getty Images; p. 18 Mark Deeble and Victoria Stone/Oxford Scientific/Getty Images; p. 19 iStockphoto/Thinkstock; p. 20 Eduardo Jose Bernardino/E+/Getty Images; p. 21 (top) KROMKRATHOG/Shutterstock.com; p. 21 (bottom) Kate Baldwin/StockFood Creative/Getty Images; p. 22 Peter Walton Photography/Photolibrary/Getty Images.

Library of Congress Cataloging-in-Publication Data

Baxter, Bethany.
 Caimans, gharials, alligators, and crocodiles / by Bethany Baxter. — 1st ed.
   pages cm. — (Awesome armored animals)
 Includes index.
 ISBN 978-1-4777-0798-2 (library binding) — ISBN 978-1-4777-0968-9 (pbk.) —
 ISBN 978-1-4777-0969-6 (6-pack)
 1. Crocodilians—Juvenile literature. I. Title.
 QL666.C9B39 2014
 597.98—dc23
                              2013000452

Manufactured in the United States of America

CPSIA Compliance Information: Batch #S13PK6: For Further Information contact Rosen Publishing, New York, New York at 1-800-237-9932

Contents

Armored Reptiles

Crocodilians are a group of reptiles that **evolved** more than 200 million years ago. They lived on Earth with the dinosaurs, yet they are still around today! Today, this group is made up of caimans, gharials, alligators, and crocodiles. Crocodilians are known for having hard, scaly skin. Their scales act like armor that helps keep them safe from animal **predators** and people.

Gharials, like the one shown here, have long, narrow snouts and lots of sharp teeth.

This is a Cuvier's dwarf caiman, the smallest crocodilian. This species lives in South America.

There are 23 **species** of crocodilians alive today. The smallest is the Cuvier's dwarf caiman. It grows to be only 5 feet (1.5 m) long as an adult. The largest is the Indopacific crocodile. Adult Indopacific crocodiles can grow to be more than 23 feet (7 m) long!

Most crocodilians live in tropical **habitats**. These places are near Earth's **equator**, where it is warm or hot all year long. Different species of crocodilians live in parts of Africa, India, Southeast Asia, Australia, North America, Central America, and South America. Sometimes crocodilians are named after the place they live, as the American alligator and Chinese crocodile are.

Alligators' coloring helps them blend into their habitats. This allows them to sneak up on prey.

Some crocodile species can live in salt water, as this saltwater crocodile can.

All crocodilians live in wet habitats, such as swamps, ponds, rivers, lakes, and marshes. They spend most of their time in the water. Crocodilians may live in salt water, freshwater, or brackish water, which is a mix of freshwater and salt water.

Caimans, gharials, alligators, and crocodiles have skin covered in hard scales and bony plates. Their scales and plates keep them safe from most people and other animals. They shed their scales one at a time instead of **molting** their skin, as snakes do. The color of many crocodilians' skin lets them blend into their habitats.

Crocodilians have many sharp teeth. Here, you can see the big teeth of this crocodile.

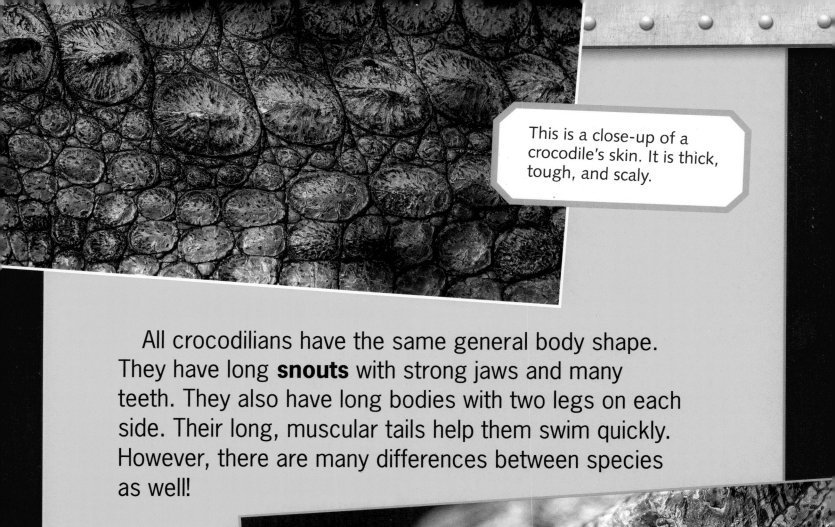

This is a close-up of a crocodile's skin. It is thick, tough, and scaly.

All crocodilians have the same general body shape. They have long **snouts** with strong jaws and many teeth. They also have long bodies with two legs on each side. Their long, muscular tails help them swim quickly. However, there are many differences between species as well!

Crocodilians have a third transparent eyelid that protects their eyes when they swim underwater.

Crocodilians are mostly solitary animals. This means they live alone as adults, instead of in groups. Crocodilians are territorial. They defend their territories, or living spaces, from others in the same habitat. Some crocodilians are more **dominant** than others. Dominant crocodilians get to pick the best territories for hunting and resting.

Here, a group of alligators is fighting.

Crocodilians **communicate** by making noises. They roar, hiss, and growl at each other. They also slap their heads and snap their jaws against the water to mark their territories. Sometimes crocodilians fight with each other over territories. They smack their heads together and bite at each other.

Crocodilian Facts!

2. To tell alligators and crocodiles apart, look at their snouts. Alligators have wide, rounded snouts. Crocodiles have narrow, more pointed snouts.

2. Crocodilians can hold their breath underwater for more than two hours, as long as they stay still and do not use up their energy.

3. Crocodilians are cold-blooded. This means they must depend on their habitats to stay warm. Crocodilians often bask in the sun to warm their bodies.

4. The black caiman is the largest predator in South America. Adult male black caimans can grow to be more than 20 feet (6 m) long!

5. Crocodilians may eat only about 50 meals a year. They can also go as long as two years without eating!

6. Crocodiles and alligators often sit with their mouths open. This is called gaping. Scientists think they may do this to cool their bodies.

Eggs and Babies

Male and female crocodilians **mate** in the water. However, female crocodilians lay their eggs on land. First, a female digs a hole in the sand or mud to make a nest. Then, she lays her eggs and covers up the nest with more sand or mud. Smaller crocodilians lay only about 10 eggs, while large species may lay up to 50 eggs. The female stays with the nest to protect the eggs from predators.

Crocodile hatchlings

This female crocodile is protecting her eggs. When they hatch, she will take the hatchlings to the water.

When the eggs start to hatch, the babies cry out. The female hears the cries and digs them out of the nest. Then, she carries the babies to the water one at a time.

Crocodilians are carnivores. This means they eat only meat. However, they are not picky eaters. They generally eat what they can find when they are hungry. Their diets include fish, snakes, turtles, frogs, and birds. Large crocodilians also hunt mammals.

Crocodilians lie still in the water until an animal comes close. Then, they attack it very quickly.

This Nile crocodile is attacking a wildebeest. Nile crocodiles are the largest crocodilians in Africa.

Crocodilians use their strong jaws and sharp teeth for biting and holding their food. However, they do not chew their food. Instead, they swallow it whole. The **acid** in crocodilians' stomachs helps them **digest** their meals, including animal shells and bones.

Crocodilians sneak up on their prey. When they are close enough they lunge out of the water and attack.

What Eats Crocodilians?

Large adult crocodilians have no animal predators. They are too big for other animals to eat! However, even smaller adult crocodilians are not in danger from other animals. They are kept safe by their hard scales, strong jaws, and fast swimming.

Mongooses, like this one, eat young crocodiles.

Crocodilians' eyes are near the tops of their heads. This lets them show only a small part of themselves when they surface.

However, crocodilian eggs and young crocodilians are often eaten by other animals. For example, lizards and foxes steal eggs from caiman nests. Young caimans are much smaller than adults. They are hunted by large fish, snakes, birds, and other crocodilians. Young crocodilians try to blend in with their habitats to keep safe from predators. They also call out to their mothers to protect them from other animals.

19

Alligators, caimans, and gharials can live for about 60 years in the wild. Crocodiles live even longer, for 75 years or more! However, many crocodilians do not live that long. They are caught and killed by humans instead. Crocodilians are hunted for their meat and skin in many parts of the world.

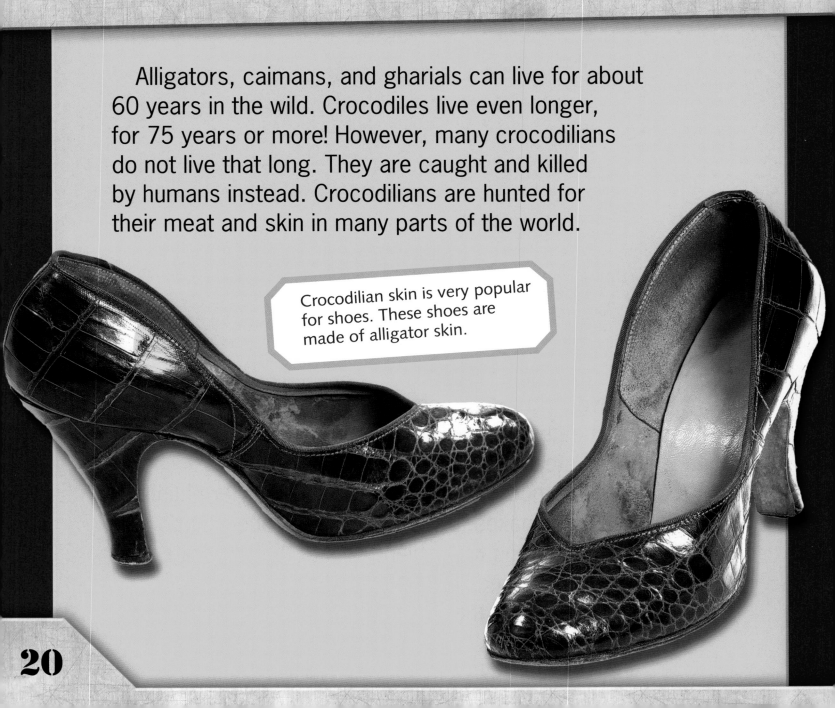

Crocodilian skin is very popular for shoes. These shoes are made of alligator skin.

People all around the world eat crocodilian meat. This woman is grilling crocodile meat in Thailand.

Their skin is used for clothing, shoes, and bags. People also collect crocodilian eggs for food. The **populations** of many crocodilian species have become very small because of hunting.

In some places, it is now against the law to hunt crocodilians. However, **poachers** continue to hunt them and sell their skins.

People in the United States eat crocodilians, too. This alligator meat was fried.

21

The Future for Crocodilians

Many species of crocodilians are in danger of dying out because of hunting. However, crocodilians are also in danger because humans are destroying their habitats. People are cutting down tropical rain forests and wetlands to build more homes and farms. When this happens, many crocodilians have no place to live.

Crocodilians have been on Earth for more than 200 million years. People must work together to keep crocodilians and their habitats safe. We want to make sure these amazing reptiles will be around for many more years to come!

Glossary

acid (A-sud) A liquid that breaks down matter faster than water does.

communicate (kuh-MYOO-nih-kayt) To share facts or feelings.

digest (dy-JEST) To break down food so that the body can use it.

dominant (DAH-mih-nent) In charge.

equator (ih-KWAY-tur) The imaginary line around Earth that separates it into two parts, northern and southern.

evolved (ih-VOLVD) Changed over many years.

habitats (HA-buh-tats) The surroundings where an animal or a plant naturally lives.

mate (MAYT) To join together to make babies.

molting (MOHLT-ing) Shedding hair, feathers, shell, horns, or skin.

poachers (POH-cherz) People who illegally kill animals that are protected by the law.

populations (pop-yoo-LAY-shunz) Groups of animals or people living in the same area.

predators (PREH-duh-terz) Animals that kill other animals for food.

snouts (SNOWTS) Long noses.

species (SPEE-sheez) A single kind of living thing. All people are one species.

Index

Websites

Due to the changing nature of Internet links, PowerKids Press has developed an online list of websites related to the subject of this book. This site is updated regularly. Please use this link to access the list: www.powerkidslinks.com/aaa/caima/